Peter

HAIGH HALL
and the Bradshaigh Family

P & D Riley

First published 2006
Reprinted 2007

P & D Riley
12 Bridgeway East
Cheshire
WA7 6LD
England

Copyright © 2006 by Peter Riley

ISBN: 1 874712 48 4
ISBN: (From January 2007) 978 1874712 48 0

British Library Cataloguing in Publication Data
A catalogue record for this book is available from the British Library

All rights reserved. No part of this publication may be reproduced, stored in a retrieval system, or transmitted, in any form or by any means, electronic, mechanical, photocopying, recording or otherwise, without the permission of the publisher and the copyright owner.

Printed in England by JPS Design & Print

Introduction

For many centuries the name Haigh Hall in Wigan has been well known to the people of the town and to those in townships for many miles around. Not only were the Bradshaigh family the major landowners of the region, but Sir William Bradshaigh who lived at the hall in the 14th century served in the crusades, so his reputation was kindled into that of having a special status.

He was evidently a fiery character and had many battles on a more local front with neighbouring landowners, as did his illustrious descendent Sir Roger Bradshaigh who took part in the dispute known as the English Civil War, supporting the restoration of King Charles II.

As can be expected, a knight of the realm was required to have a huge house in those heady days of flaunting wealth and power, and Haigh Hall was the result. It is a large property that in its time has seen servants, gardeners and many influential people tread its paths and corridors, including that lovable royal rogue King Edward VII and his wife Queen Alexandra when they were the Prince and Princess of Wales. This proves that the influence of the Haigh household existed until fairly recent times. Alas, times change and fortunes with them, and in 1947 Wigan Council bought the hall and surrounding lands and made them into the popular public park they are today.

It is to be hoped that this modest book will allow readers to enjoy the history of this treasure of Wigan's long past.

Peter Riley

Acknowledgements

The author would like to thank the following for their help during the preparation of this book

Moira Fry of Haigh Hall Information Centre
Gary Powell, Duty Manager at Haigh Hall
Rev. Ray Hutchinson, Rector of Wigan Parish Church
Wigan Archives Services
Manchester Local Studies Library

By the same author in this series

Wythenshawe Hall and the Tatton family
Heaton Hall and the Egerton Family
Bramall Hall and the Davenport Family
Crewe Hall and the Crewe Family

ONE

The history of Haigh Hall can be traced back for many centuries, at least as far back as 1188, during the last year in the reign of Henry II and the closing years of the 12th century. In that year Haigh was in the possession of Hugh Le Norreys. At the time England was in turmoil. The king was under pressure from his sons Richard and John to abandon the throne, and Richard, the eldest, ultimately succeeded his father as the famous Richard the Lionheart.

Elsewhere in England the country was in a period of strife, with local barons and landowners at each others throats. In fact it was a dangerous time to be living in England, with peasants living hand to mouth in clearings in the huge forests that then covered most of the country. Early reports show that in Anglo-Saxon times the average price of a cow was four shillings and sixpence, a sheep one shilling and two pence and a pig one shilling and elevenpence, while a horse, which relied on hay and corn to live cost around one pound, five shillings, a figure far beyond the resources of an average citizen.

In Lancashire the danger to ordinary people was particularly bad, with landowners within the county in a state of perpetual war over claims and counterclaims that they were stealing each other's horses and other livestock and generally terrorising everyone by sending out bands of armed men to inflict summary 'justice' to those they caught unlawfully on their land. There was also trouble in the county from marauding Scots who seemed to roam into Lancashire and take what they wanted without much opposition.

Into this scenario, then, we see Haigh Hall at the centre of life around Wigan, then a small hamlet on the fringes of the kingdoms of Mercia and Northumberland, the two main feudal kingdoms in the north of England.

Little is known about the Le Norreys but we must speculate that they were quite wealthy, for they undoubtedly mixed on a higher social level than the average person in the area, for Haigh is recorded as becoming in 1295 the property of Hugh Le Norreys grandson, also called Hugh, and subsequently into the possession of his daughter Mabel who married Sir William de Bradshaigh, a family of Anglo-Saxon origin.

This marriage was the start of centuries of ownership by the Bradshaigh family, but the marriage of Mabel to Sir William also brought a touch of drama, indeed legend, to the history of Haigh. At the time of the marriage England was again torn apart by strife, was at war with the Scots, and the Crusades were well under way in the Middle East.

Legend tells us he was away from Haigh Hall from 1315 until 1322 and during his years of absence Mabel believed that he had been killed and, after a decent period of mourning, married a Welsh knight. The legend continues that Sir William returned to Wigan in disguise (though no reason is given for this) and as he mixed with the poor of the town he was spotted by Mabel who was so overcome at the sight of this peasant who looked so much like her late husband that she was very distressed. This in turn angered the Welsh knight (named in one account written in 1564 by Sir William Norris of Speke as Sir Henry Teuther) who turned his wrath on Mabel in a fit of jealousy.

Sir William then made himself known to his tenants and the knight fled in fear and astonishment, closely pursued by Sir William. The chase took them to Newton-le-Willows where Sir William overtook his rival and killed him at a spot still known today as the Bloody Stone, close to the present Newton-le-Willows railway station.

Because of her mistake in 'marrying' the Sir Henry, Lady Mabel was made to do penance by walking once a week barefoot from Haigh Hall to the market cross in Standishgate, in Wigan village centre.

Sir William Bradshaigh himself was outlawed for a year and a day for killing his rival, but upon his return to Haigh Hall it seems that he and Lady Mabel lived happily together for the rest of their lives, and even today they rest in peace together within the holy confines of Wigan Parish Church where there is still an effigy of them in repose above the family tomb on the north side of the chapel altar.

Where Lady Mabel concluded her weekly walk became known locally as Mab's Cross and it still exists in the grounds of a local school where it was removed from the public highway in 1921 with the expansion of Wigan traffic.

The entrance hall at Haigh

According to some accounts the exploits of Sir William Bradshaigh were many and varied, and he was undoubtedly a fiery character. Historians have recorded that the reason for Sir William's long absence from Haigh Hall and Lady Mabel was an upheaval in Lancashire caused by the overbearing attitude of Sir Robert de Holland, a favourite of the Earl of Lancaster, who had risen to power and prestige through his influence. Acting on behalf of the Earl, Sir Robert held dictatorial powers over the people of Lancashire, including the power of life and death. His relatives, though not having direct power of their own, abused their connection to Sir Robert and became generally arrogant.

An early contemporary print of Haigh Hall

This caused dissent among local gentry in the county and soon there was hatred and jealousy levelled against Sir Roger. Sir William de Bradshaigh and Sir Adam Banastre gathered together a band of like minded men and staged a revolt which quickly got out of hand. During one conflict another of Sir William's enemies, Sir Henry de Bury, was killed. An inquiry followed and Sir William was outlawed for not appearing in court while some of his supporters were sentenced to death for murder and hanged.

Sir Adam Banastre, undettered by the changing circumstances, rallied a force of 800 men around him, including Sir William, and raided many parts of Lancashire, pillaging farms and wealthy houses until a force of militiamen was ordered to pursue them by the Sheriff.

Many of those in the company of Sir Adam Banastre and Sir William de Bradshaigh fled but were subsequently captured and killed. Sir William was one of the luckier ones for he managed to escape. Although he was pardoned in 1318 he decided to remain clear of Haigh Hall while the county still remained unstable and so many of his enemies continued to dominate the region. It was thus assumed by those who wished him harm, and by Lady Mabel herself, that he had died in trying to escape and we can only imagine the shock of his return to Wigan four years later.

The reason for his return in 1322 was

Mab's Cross in Victorian days

simple: his arch enemy the Earl of Lancaster had been executed for treason, while the Earl's arrogant favourite, Sir Robert de Holland, had been imprisoned and deprived of all his possessions. However, this did not mean that Wigan was safe, for Sir Robert had many friends in the area who would have liked nothing better than to see Sir William de Bradshaigh killed. They did in fact attack Haigh Hall on at least one occasion but were driven off or killed. Despite defending his home it appears that Sir William was arrested but released on payment of a fine.

   His return to Haigh Hall lasted no more than five years and in 1333 Sir William de Bradshaigh was killed in Newton-le-Willows and legend says he was killed on the very spot (the Bloody Stone) where he had killed the Welsh knight.

   Lady Mabel lived for a further fifteen years after Sir William and died in 1348. There has been much speculation about the story of Mab's Cross, but it appears that the penance story was true, though the legend that the cross in Standishgate that bears her name was only constructed after her exploits is certainly untrue, for records show that there was a cross in Standishgate many years before she was born, and it is interesting to note that in a deed dating from 1403 it was called Mabcrosse.

   Historian H.H.G. Arthur, writing in his book *A History of Haigh Hall* (1952) wrote: "Crosses were regarded in those days as a symbol of expressing sorrow for sin. The route she took from Haigh to the cross can only be a matter for conjecture, but she probably chose the most private path, which would be along the banks of the River Douglas until level with the cross, and not

Bradshaigh Coat of Arms

down Wigan Lane."

After the death of Lady Mabel, Haigh Hall passed to a nephew of her late husband though not before another legend was born, for it is said that the ghost of Mabel haunted a gallery in the old hall which became known as Mab's Galley, and even novelist Sir Walter Scott, writing almost five hundred years later, mentioned the tale in his famous work *Waverley* which was published in 1814.

TWO

In Tudor times the wealth of Haigh Hall was derived mainly from the production of Cannel, a fuel which was regarded as a type of sea coal and which was useful for the production of gas, and its production and sale contributed greatly to the cash available for building Haigh Hall in a much more lavish style, and it is rumoured that some of the design alterations and additions to the house were supervised by noted Elizabethan architect Inigo Jones.

Whoever supervised the job there is no doubt that the Bradshaigh family deemed it necessary to keep up with their wealthy neighbours throughout Lancashire and an elaborate facade was built and a huge carved door added to the entrance, making the house altogether more impressive to those approaching it from the great drive.

Despite the wealth of Haigh Hall, the Bradshaigh family seemed to find it difficult to stay out of conflicts and Sir Roger Bradshaigh, who inherited the estate in 1641 while in his early teens, found himself embroiled in the second Civil War as a fervent Royalist.

In 1650 after the heir to the throne, Charles II, landed in Scotland intending to claim the throne back following his exile in France after the execution of Charles I, Sir Roger Bradshaigh found himself under arrest. His future could have been very bleak or even non-existent but the judiciary of the time took a lenient view of his involvement and released him on an understanding that he would no longer assist the Royalist cause.

The conflict did not disappear however, and the Earl of Derby was determined to take Lancashire with his Royalist army but his forces were intercepted at Wigan Lane where a major battle took place and the Earl's forces were defeated, though he managed to escape. The fortunes of other Royalists, however, were mixed, and one of them, Sir Thomas Tyldesley from Leigh, eight miles from Wigan, was killed and a monument was later erected in his memory in Wigan Lane. Sir Roger Bradshaigh had apparently kept out of the way while the battle was going on but afterwards it was reported that he had travelled to the scene of the conflict and managed to rescue fellow Royalist Sir William Throgmorton, who had been left for dead, and returned with him to Haigh Hall.

The Civil War in Lancashire went poorly for the Royalist cause and the Earl of Derby was eventually captured and taken to Bolton where he was executed by being beheaded in the town centre in full public gaze.

However, as history shows, the Royalist cause triumphed eventually with the restoration to the throne of Charles II and by way of thanks the king granted a new Charter to Wigan making it a borough, with Sir Roger Bradshaigh of Haigh Hall named as the town's new Mayor.

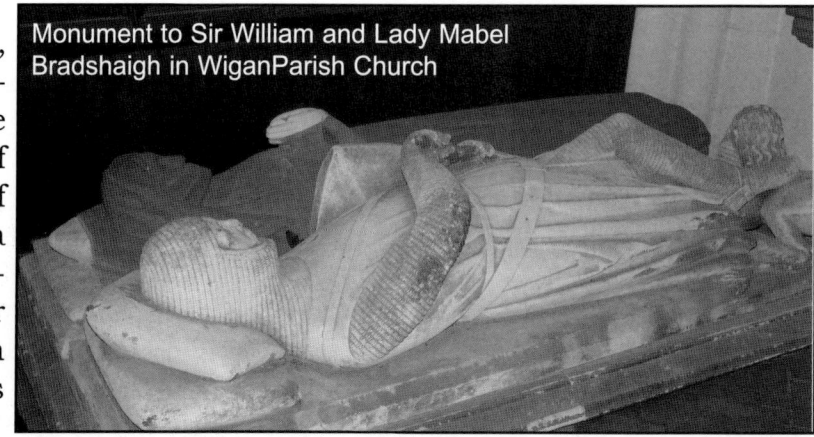

Sketch of monument to Sir Thomas Tyldesley

Monument to Sir William and Lady Mabel Bradshaigh in Wigan Parish Church

Sir Roger Bradshaigh with his wife Dorothy, whom he married in 1746

Following restoration of peace to England it soon became necessary for landowners to boost their finances, many of which had been badly depleted during the Civil War periods and Sir Roger Bradshaigh was no exception. He, however, was in a more fortunate position than many of his contemporaries in Lancashire and set about developing his profitable cannel mines. What was not properly taken into consideration however was the enormous expense of improvements necessary to make the mining operation work efficiently and Sir Roger started to develop a major drainage scheme which became known locally as the Wigan Great Sough.

By this scheme it was possible for mine workings and nearby land to be drained of unwanted water effectively as major flooding had often caused major mining difficulties. Sir Roger developed a unique underground tunnel which drained his mines into Yellow Brook at a point where it joined the River Douglas, though the scheme took 18 years to complete and cost a fortune. It was regarded in its day as an astounding feat of engineering since it was almost a mile in length and relied on common sense during its construction since no proper geological knowledge existed at that time. What is so fascinating is that this unique system, known to this day as Wigan Great Sough, still drains water from the former workings of the Haigh estate

Yellow Brook Waterfall, Wigan Great Sough, Haigh

more than three centuries later.

The enormous cost of the Sough and extracting the cannel of Haigh was to cause a major financial problem for the family and after his death in 1684 his son who inherited the estate found his finances strained and it has been speculated on whether the strain of trying to keep Haigh Hall and its estate working was the cause of his death only two years after Sir Roger.

The name Sir Roger Bradshaigh was in common use within the family for almost two hundred years, the last one dying in 1770, when the estate was inherited by his sister's granddaughter, ten years old Elizabeth Dalrymple, for whom it was held in trust until she married Alexander Lindsay, 23rd Earl of Crawford, when she was twenty years old.

Below: Haigh Hall in the 18th century

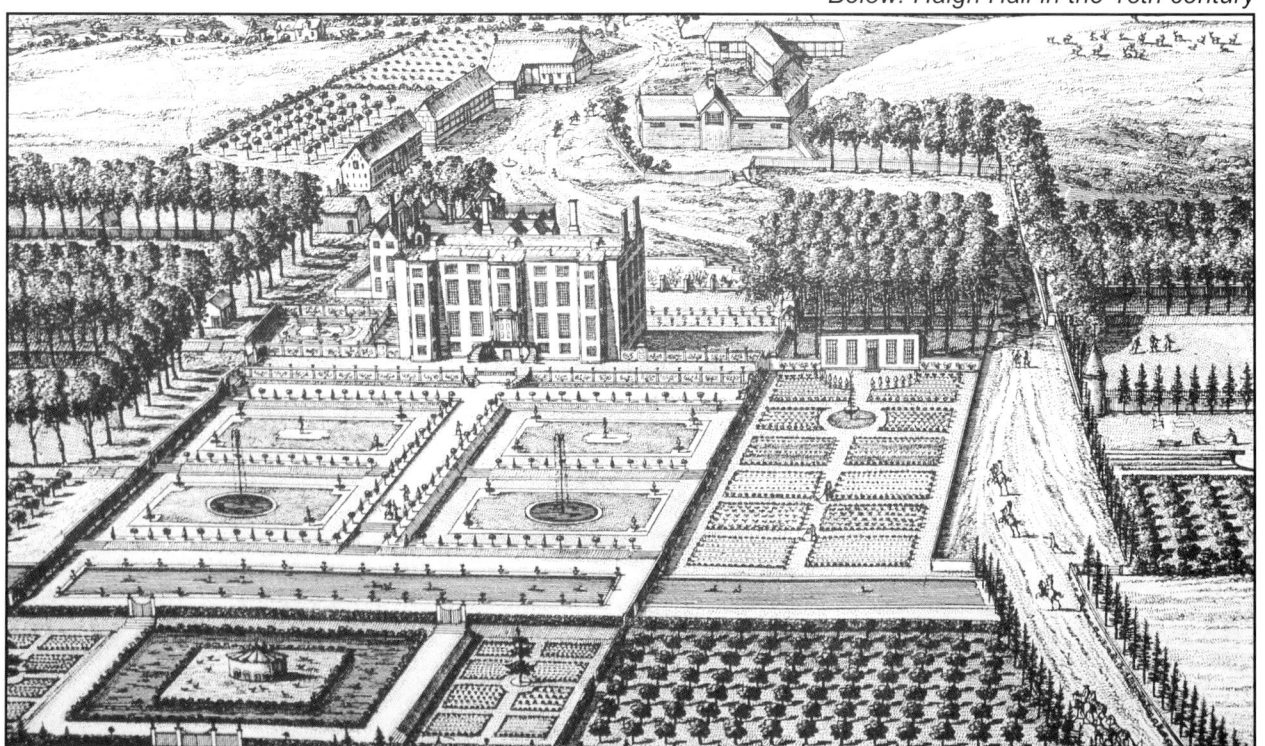

Haigh Hall as it looks today

THREE

From hereon the Lindsay family took control of Haigh Hall and the extensive estate, and their family name and the Earl of Crawford title became the common currency among local people and fellow landowners in and around Wigan.

The title Earl of Crawford has one of the longest lineages in Britain, dating back to 1398 when Sir David Lindsay was given the peerage in Scotland as the first Earl by Robert II.

The title descended from one descendant to the next, and like many other families there were skeletons in the cupboard, including a tale dating from the 1540s. In 1542 David Lindsay, the 8th Earl, died and his title should have been taken by his son Alexander, who was nicknamed *The Wicked Master* because of his quarrelsome and aggressive nature. In fact he was so aggressive that he had tried to murder his father and had been sentenced to death for the attempt. Thus the title of 9th Earl of Crawford was instead bestowed on his cousin, also called David Lindsay, and it was deemed that all descendants of *The Wicked Master* would be excluded from carrying the title.

The 9th Earl, however, had ideas of his own and he evidently decided that the lineage should be returned to its rightful line of descent, and though he had sons of his own who would be expected to have succeeded to the title he decreed that on his death the Earldom would go to yet another David Lindsay, son of The Wicked Master.

In 1558 the 8th Earl died and the line of descent thus returned to the mainstream of the Lindsay family, though the 9th Earl was afterwards referred to as an interpolated Earl!

By 1652, upon the death of Ludovic Lindsay, the 16th Earl, the family title was passed on to his cousin John Lindsay, who already been given the title 1st Earl of Lindsay 10 years earlier, thus the head of the family now held two names, or rather titles, a situation that continued unthwarted until the death in 1808 of George Lindsay, 22nd Earl of Crawford and 6th Earl of Lindsay, when the title became dormant until it was passed to another family line and Alexander Lindsay, who already held the title Earl of Balcarres also became the 23rd Earl of Crawford.

The grand staircase in Haigh Hall

Upon Alexander taking over the Haigh estate and hall he may have had some moments of reflection on what sort of an inheritance he had been given, for he found Haigh Hall in a state of disrepair as it had not been lived in for a decade and it had also been badly disturbed by mining subsidence.

On inspecting the estate he found run down farm buildings, dereliction in his cannel mines and hardly any income being generated, but he was a determined man who had already proved his worth in Scotland after he had inherited the Balcarres estates when he was only fourteen years old. He had, nevertheless, worked at caring for his brothers and sisters and saw the family fortunes grow.

After inheriting Haigh Hall he decided to concentrate his efforts in the Wigan area and sold his Balcarres estates to one of his brothers who had been fortunate enough to make a fortune in India.

The 23rd Earl of Crawford set about changing the fortunes at Haigh with the same determination he had shown in his earlier years and his first task was to stop the continuing subsidence which he did through building buttresses on the house. Having inherited the cannel mining operation, the Earl, who was the first to admit he know nothing about the business, nevertheless set about to increase his knowledge and even experimented with cannel in his bedroom grate.

Haigh Hall in 1850

He also realised the potential of the growing canal system in Lancashire and decided that was the best and cheapest method of transporting his fuel. He looked at the success of the Bridgewater Canal project in Worsley and decided that he

The West Library at Haigh Hall in the early 20th century

would invest in the Leeds-Liverpool Canal which ran through the Haigh estate. His confidence was so high that he purchased thirty three barges and boats.

Historian H.H.G. Arthur, in his *A History of Haigh Hall*, wrote: "Earl Alexander also considered that metal was inseparable from coal. He found that his workshops at Haigh were not large enough to cope with the manufacture of colliery machinery and all the other engineering work on his estate, so he started the Haigh Ironworks in 1790. The works began to supply other pits, one of the most notable achievements being the construction, under the supervision of Mr. Robert Daglish, of the first locomotive used in Lancashire, which was built in 1812 to convey coal at Orrell colliery, and was capable of dragging 20 wagons each containing a ton of coal. It was known locally as Daglish's Walking Horse."

Alexander died in 1825 and Haigh Hall passed to his son James Lindsay, who, at 42 years of age, became the 24th Earl of Crawford and 7th Earl of Balcarres. A decade after taking over the estate, James decided the iron works were not profitable so he leased them for 21 years, thus the Haigh Foundry Company, a wonderful training ground for many future engineers in Wigan, was born.

James, who also had the additional title of Baron Wigan of Haigh Hall, was also responsible for building the present hall which stands on the site of an hotchpotch house which dated back to Norman times with later additions made during the time of Elizabeth I.

It took almost nineteen years to build Haigh Hall and during his long exile into smaller quarters the Earl lived in Park Cottages on his estate. At times it must have seemed as if the new hall was never going to be completed, but the Earl continued enthusiastically with his supervision of the work, having drawn up the plans for the new house himself, and eventually it was completed in 1849.

But how did he pay for all this work? The answer appears to be his cannel workings which were highly profitable. There is no doubt that the Earl was an astute businessman, for during the 1860s when there was a false scare that

Looking down the main staircase

England's massive coal supplies were in danger of running out, the Earl stepped in and sold cannel while the panic continued, thus making greater profits. It is reported that much of the cannel was shipped to the USA and South America where it was used to manufacture gas for many of their cities.

Haigh Hall was built with a hard sandstone quarried in Lancashire and shipped to the site by canal where it was cut into the required shapes by steam powered saws. Iron work used in the construction also came from the Haigh Foundry, while additional furniture such as doors, including the front doors, were brought from Jamaica where James owned plantations dating back to a time when he was also Governor of that British colony, with the hall fireplaces being bought and shipped from Paris.

There is no doubt that James, the 24th Earl, was extremely popular and gave generously to local causes and his abilities and enthusiasm was widely applauded in Wigan. He invented many things for use in the hall, including windows that fitted into draughtproof steel slots which were impossible to open from the outside, while internal doors were hung on special hinges allowing them to swing through a full half circle. It was an ingenious collection of an active mind and among his further successes was a central heating system created from a combination of hot air and open fires, an unheard of luxury in those cold Victorian days!

FOUR

James died in 1869 and his son, Alexander William Crawford Lindsay, became the 25th Earl of Crawford and 8th Earl of Balcarres. This Earl had a taste for the Victorian high life and when an invitation to stay at Haigh Hall was accepted in 1873 by the Prince and Princess of Wales (later King Edward VII and Queen Alexander) during a visit to Wigan to open the Royal Albert Edward Infirmary, the house was completely redecorated at the enormous cost of £80,000.

Lady Crawford took on the mantle or organising the redecoration and ordered a London firm to carry out the work within a month! She also ordered Italian curtains and crimson and black Indian carpets, while special Spanish chairs, upholstered in leather and gold were placed in the entrance hall.

Historian H.H.G. Arthur tells us: "The morning room furniture was upholstered in velvet and silk. The long library, which is the large room on the ground floor overlooking the canal, became the banqueting hall. The sideboard was covered with gold plate. The dining chairs were crimson and green, except those used by the Royal personages, which were of silk and gold...

"Three rooms on the first floor enjoy the view across the estate to

The 'Plantation' gates to Haigh Hall estate in 1895

Wigan: an ante-room, the drawing room and the boudoir. The boudoir was specially decorated for the Princess in white and gold. The floor was covered with Persian carpets, the amber curtains were of Italian silk, the furniture was upholstered in velvet, while an ebony grand piano completed the arrangements for the Princess;s private comfort.

"The drawing room was, perhaps, the masterpiece of this artistic interior decoration, with its Persian and Turkey carpets, curtains specially woven from France, its grand piano, elegant chairs, marqueterie tables and cabinets, graced with at least 30 vases of flowers, and 80 paintings by Old Masters, including Botticelli, van Dyck, and Sir Joshua Reynolds."

The extravagance and expense of this visit would not have pleased everyone in Wigan, where the average person struggled to survive on a pittance but there appeared to be no animosity shown towards the Royal couple even after members of the public were allowed to view the Royal apartments, for a fee of sixpence, for three days after the prince and princess had left, the proceeds being donated by the Earl and Lady Crawford to the new Infirmary.

The period of the 25th Earl's occupation of Haigh Hall came at the height of the imperial British Empire and landowners were expected to spend huge amounts in entertaining and in retaining a large domestic staff and Alexander was certainly no exception for at Haigh he employed a cook, several maids, footmen, a carpenter, a plumber, a dozen grooms and coachmen and numerous odd-job men.

The Earl also kept twenty horses on his estate which consisted of forty farms all managed by a bailiff, though most were eventually let to tenant farmers. The estate was completely self-sufficient in food and fuel.

It was a huge undertaking by Earl Alexander, an accomplished author and traveller who loved books and was responsible for creating a huge library at Haigh Hall, long regarded in its time as the largest private library in England. As a great traveller he was also often away from Wigan on visits to Europe and it was during a trip to Florence that he died in 1880.

His body was brought from Italy back to Britain and was interred beneath a private mortuary chapel at Dunecht, Aberdeenshire, Scotland, where it was expected to rest for eternity. However that was not the case, and two years after his death it was discovered that the Earl's body had been stolen from the family vault. Police had no clues and private detectives who were brought in to help were also puzzled.

Despite this, however, the family decided not to offer a reward in case it should spark off a wave of similar incidents and it was not until a man named Soutar, a local ratcatcher, came forward to confess his part in helping to dispose of the Earl's body that the case was solved.

Soutar told police that he had helped bury the body in a copse though denied having any part in snatching it from the family vault. He offered to show where the body had been placed and he led them to the spot.

The *Illustrated London News* wrote: "There the late Earl's body was found, as the ratcatcher had said, and was reverently taken up and carried back to the chapel. It is to be finally deposited in the old family mausoleum at Haigh Hall, Wigan, in Lancashire.

"Soutar has been committed for trial, and there is now some hope that his statement, with other evidence, may yet lead to the apprehension of the

Recovering the body of Earl Crawford

more guilty persons. The Queen has sent a message to the Earl of Crawford and Balcarres, expressing her satisfaction that the body of his father is recovered."

It seems ironic that after spending such a fortune on the earlier visit of the Prince and Princess of Wales the 26th Earl of Crawford, James Ludovic Lindsay, should find the family fortunes declining because of a trade slump, including less demand for his cannel. Because of this the cash-strapped Earl was forced to sell some of the family possessions. In 1886 the Earl, a keen amateur astronomer, also became owner of the family estate in Balcarres but decided to sell it two years later intending to build an observatory in Edinburgh.

David, the 27th Earl of Crawford and his family pictured in 1906

He died in 1913 to be succeeded by David Alexander Edward Lindsay, who became the 27th Earl of Crawford and 10th Earl of Balcarres. It was under the ownership of the 27th Earl that the wind of change was blowing through the Haigh estate. Only a year after taking his inheritance Britain was plummeted into the horrors of the First World War and Haigh Hall found itself being used as a military hospital, coping with casualties brought back to Blighty from devastated Belgium and France.

The former stables at Haigh Hall as they look today.

Inset: David, the 27th Earl of Crawford

In 1918 after the armistice, Britain was never the same again and the old time gentry died out. Those who had doffed caps and been servants to landowners prior to the war either failed to return due to the huge casualty figures or decided that this "Land fit for Heroes" as the British Government called it, was not the place to doff caps any longer and across the country, including Haigh Hall, the pattern of life was changed.

Despite attempts to retain some order, the onset of the Second World War was the final straw and in 1940, at the height of the threat to England, the 27th Earl died, leaving Haigh Hall and parkland to his son David Alexander Robert Lindsay, who, aged 40, became the 28th Earl of Crawford and 11th Earl of Balcarres.

The 'Plantation' gates to Haigh Hall as they look today.

In 1947, as austerity hit Wigan and other parts of the nation, Wigan Corporation bought Haigh Hall and its estate and a year later opened them up to the public. The 28th Earl of Crawford, who died in 1975, retained his titles upto his death and even today the titles remain in the Lindsay family. The current (29th) Earl of Crawford is Robert Alexander Lindsay, who also continues to retain the Scottish historic connection as the 12th Earl of Balcarres, and he has a son, Anthony Robert Lindsay, born in 1958, who is heir apparent to the titles and already has one of his own as Lord Balniel.

Today Haigh Hall retains a touch of class and has many elaborate rooms, though nothing like its former splendour, but is no longer open to the public. Instead it is hired out for weddings and other functions, though the park itself is still extremely popular all year round and it is undoubtedly the jewel in the crown of Wigan.

Bibliography

A History of Haigh Hall by H.H.G. Arthur (1952)
Description of the Country from 30 to 40 miles around Manchester by John Aiken (1795)
Lancashire Faces and Places (previously *Manchester Faces and Places*),
a series of magazines published from 1889 until 1914
Hutchinson's *Story of the British Nation* (4 volumes - 1924))
Lancashire Halls by Margaret Chapman (1971)
The History of Lancashire - Vol IV, (1891) by Edward Baines
Traditions of Lancashire (1882)
Memorials of Old Lancashire, Vol 2. by Fishwick & Ditchfield (1909)

Photo Album

Above: A traditional highly carved wooden seat still seen in the hall

Right: The Long Gallery as it looks today

Top: One side of Haigh Hall, giving an impression of its huge size

Bottom left: The Long Gallery with its ornate ceiling

Bottom right: The Grand Ballroom

Top left: A sketch of Wigan Parish Church as it looked in the Victorian era. This was the place of worship for the Bradshaigh family

Top right: A packhorse bridge and canal in Haigh village, once used for transporting Cannel

Bottom: The Crawford family name is remembered in this Haigh inn, *The Crawford Arms*